DOLPHINS

Bottle-nose dolphins perform at Sea World in San Diego, California. Aphrodite (first from the right) is the highest jumping bottle-nose dolphin in the world. She can lift her 600 pounds 23 feet out of the water. (Sea World)

A FIRST BOOK

DOLPHINS

by Martha and Robert Moffett

ILLUSTRATED WITH PHOTOGRAPHS

Franklin Watts, Inc.
845 Third Avenue
New York, N.Y. 10022

Cover photograph (courtesy
United Press International)
shows a baby dolphin
swimming right next to
his proud-looking mother.

SBN 531-00723-5
Copyright © 1971 by Franklin Watts, Inc.
Library of Congress Catalog Card Number: 76-134497
Printed in the United States of America
4 5 6

CONTENTS

Meet the Dolphin	3
The Dolphin Is a Mammal	4
The Dolphin's Family Tree	6
The Dolphin's Relatives	7
Different Dolphins	11
What Dolphins Are Like	19
The Senses of the Dolphin	29
The Important Sense of Sound	34
The Language of the Dolphin	42
The Young Dolphin	48
Dolphin Society	55
Man Meets Dolphin	58
Performing Dolphins	61
Scientists Become Curious	64
A Dolphin Joins the Navy	66
How to Catch a Dolphin	67
How Intelligent Is the Dolphin?	69
The Dolphin's Brain	73
Current Research on Dolphins	76
Conversation with a Dolphin	79
Index	83

DOLPHINS

MEET THE DOLPHIN

Have you ever talked to an animal? Of course you have. You give commands to your dog or you call your cat. And they understand at least a few words. You have communicated with them. But it is one-way communication. Dogs and cats do not answer because they do not have a language. And even if they were intelligent enough to learn your language, they would still be physically unable to speak.

But there is one animal that has all the things necessary to communicate with man.

This animal has the intelligence — his brain is actually larger than man's. He can make many of the sounds that man uses. He can even make sounds that are impossible for human beings to hear. And, most important, he may have his own language.

This animal is the dolphin. Right now, scientists around the world are working to find a way of talking with him. They are discovering that this fishlike creature (that is not a fish) has a great many things in common with man. These things give scientists hope that two-way communication will be possible. Scientists are also discovering very special differences between man and dolphin.

The first step in learning to talk with these amazing animals is to learn all about them — what they are, how they live, and how they think.

The smiling dolphin has a brain larger than man's.
(Marineland of the Pacific, Los Angeles)

THE DOLPHIN IS A MAMMAL

One thing the dolphin has in common with man is that, despite his fishlike looks, he is a mammal.

A mammal is a vertebrate, which means that he has a backbone. This makes him one of the higher animals, along with the fish, amphibians, reptiles, and birds.

A mammal is warm-blooded. His inside body temperature remains the same no matter what the weather outside may be. If the weather becomes so cold or so hot as to affect his delicately balanced body temperature, he could die. Birds are also warm-blooded. But fish, amphibians, and reptiles are cold-blooded. Their bodies change temperature with the climate.

There are two important things that set mammals apart from all the other classes of animal life. These two things are *hair* and *glands*. The glands make it possible for the mother to give the baby milk.

It doesn't matter whether the animal walks on the land, flies, or swims. If he has both hair and glands, he is a mammal. There are more than fifteen thousand known species of mammals. Some mammals — the bats — can fly. There are even mammals, such as the platypus, that lay eggs. But nobody mistakes them for birds. Both the bat and the platypus have hair and milk glands.

And so it is with the dolphin. He spends his entire life in the sea, but he is definitely a mammal. He may look smooth and slick, but if you examine him closely, you will find a few short hairs around his mouth, like the whiskers of a cat. And, difficult as it

The dolphin looks smooth and slick. (Marineland of the Pacific, Los Angeles)

may seem for an animal that lives in the water, the mother dolphin does feed her young milk.

THE DOLPHIN'S FAMILY TREE

The dolphin is a mammal, but he is different from most other mammals. Why? We must look far back in time for the answer.

Until about 400 million years ago, the sea was filled with life, but nothing lived on the land. Then plants spread from the sea and covered the earth. This provided food for other forms of life. Fossils — preserved remains of animals and plants — show us that about 300 million years ago, some bony fish began to develop lungs. The lungs made it possible for them to breathe air.

From these early creatures, new life-forms evolved that were better suited to living on land. The first were the amphibians, animals that live both in water and on land. They usually have gills when young and lungs when they are adult. The reptiles, cold-blooded animals born with lungs, were next.

While the giant reptiles, the dinosaurs, still ruled the earth — some 125 million years ago — a small creature developed that was the first mammal. From these tiny insect-eaters descended all the great orders of mammals. With the disappearance of the dinosaurs, mammals began to evolve rapidly into many, many forms.

Competition for food on the land became more and more fierce. Gradually, some of the mammals began to spend large parts of their lives in the water. The sea, which their ancestors had left in search of food on the land, became their hunting ground.

THE DOLPHIN'S RELATIVES

One group of mammals that took to the sea were the ancestors of the present order of Cetacea (see-*tay*-sha). This order includes whales, porpoises, and dolphins.

We do not know what these early cetacean ancestors looked like. Their fossils have never been discovered. But we do know their bodies gradually changed shape until they began to resemble fish. The reason for this is easy to see. A fish shape is the best form for moving fast in water. (Man has applied this lesson in building ships and submarines.)

Readapting to life in the water is a long, slow process. Some modern mammals are going through it today. Seals, otters, and walruses still spend part of their lives on land. But if they continue to evolve as the cetaceans did, they will eventually leave the land altogether for a life in the sea.

Three different suborders of cetaceans eventually developed. One was the archaeocetes (*ar*-ke-o-*set*-ese). These strange, long, snakelike animals were an unsuccessful experiment of nature, and they disappeared around 25 million years ago. The two surviving groups — the Mysticeti (mis-te-*set*-eye) and the Odontoceti (o-*don*-to-set-eye) — are the whales, dolphins, and porpoises of today.

The huge Mysticeti — cetaceans without teeth — cruise the seas of the world. They live mostly on tiny relatives of the shrimp, which they strain through curtains of baleen. Baleen is an adaptation of the ridges you can feel with your tongue on the roof of your mouth. Although the blue whale is the largest creature on earth, he must strain his food in this way because his throat is too small to swallow anything much bigger than the little crustaceans.

Scientists believe that the Odontoceti, or toothed whales — the suborder to which the dolphins and porpoises belong — descended from a different ancestor than the Mysticeti. All the Odontoceti are carnivores. The largest, the sperm whale, dives as deep as 500 fathoms (3,000 feet) to kill the great squid on which he feeds.

Dolphins and porpoises are the smallest members of the whale family. Dolphins can be identified by their beaked noses. Porpoises have blunt noses. Dolphins belong to the family Delphinidae (del-*fin*-i-day) and porpoises to the family Phocaenidae (foe-*can*-i-day).

Dolphins are much better known than porpoises. This is not because there is any shortage of porpoises or because men are not

Teeth of a killer whale.
(United Press International)

Dolphins remain calm when lifted out of water. (United Press International)

interested in studying them. The reason is that both dolphins and porpoises will die if they are unconscious for more than a few moments. Scientists have tried to capture porpoises. But as soon as the porpoises have been lifted out of the water, they have gone into shock and died. For some reason not yet understood, dolphins remain calm when handled in this way. With proper care, they can survive long trips, and so they offer man the chance to get to know them better.

DIFFERENT DOLPHINS

When someone talks about "people," most of us think we know what he means. In our minds we picture humans who look and live much the way we do. But we could be very wrong.

There are great differences among human beings. The Eskimo not only has a way of life quite different from someone living in more temperate lands, but his body has evolved to make him better suited to that life. The Congo Pygmy can survive conditions that would quickly kill the Eskimo. But the Pygmy would face terrible survival problems if he lived farther south, in the Kalihari Desert where the Bushman lives. Each is suited to his own way of life. And yet all of them — all of us — are people.

These great differences exist among dolphins. Until you explain what kind of dolphin you are talking about, you have not really told anyone very much, for there are many kinds of dolphins. Just the word "dolphin" does not tell how big he is, what he eats, or where he lives in the world. It is as though a dolphin were describing people in this way: "They live out of the water and get around on two poles and seem to be fairly smart."

To make things even more complicated, some fish are called dolphins. They are, of course, no relative of the dolphins we are talking about. So that people would not think they were talking about the fish, many Americans have incorrectly called the dolphin a porpoise.

What most of us think of when we hear the word "dolphin" is the *bottle-nose dolphin,* often called the common porpoise. He is the dolphin who in recent years has entertained people, first in shows at places like Marineland in Florida, then later on television. He may be the smartest of his family.

The bottle-nose is found in all the oceans of the world. He grows to a length of 12 feet but averages around 8 feet, with a weight of almost 350 pounds. In their wild state, bottle-nose dolphins live in large schools, feeding on tiny fish, shrimps, and small squid known as cuttlefish. In captivity, a bottle-nose is fed up to 22 pounds of fish a day. Although he is charming and friendly, the constant smile on his face has nothing to do with how he feels. It is his normal expression. It might seem odd to us, but he wears the same smile even when he is angry.

A young bottle-nose.
(Marineland of the Pacific, Los Angeles)

The killer whale. (Marineland of the Pacific, Los Angeles)

The most dangerous animal on earth — that is how some people have described the largest member of the dolphin family. And his name suits his role — *killer whale*. One of his nicknames is sea wolf. There is good reason for this. The killer whale is a large dolphin (up to 30 feet long) who hunts in packs of from 5 to 40 animals. They are capable of attacking and killing the blue whale. But they will eat almost any creature that is unlucky enough to cross their paths — other dolphins, penguins, seals, and large fish.

They will attack walruses, but are careful of the fully grown male walrus with his long tusks and great strength.

The killer whale combines power (he can make 40-foot leaps, 4 feet out of the water), intelligence, and cooperation. No other sea animal has a defense against him. Seals sleeping on the ice are tipped into the water by killer whales ramming the ice floe. These whales are the only natural enemy of the other cetaceans. The stomach of a 21-foot killer whale was found to contain 13 porpoises and 14 seals. Killer whales are capable of swallowing 30 seals at one meal.

The *false killer* — he grows to only 18 feet — is sometimes

The false killer. (Marineland of the Pacific, Los Angeles)

A pilot whale is lowered into the water. (Marineland of the Pacific, Los Angeles)

A small common dolphin and a huge killer whale play together in a tank at Marineland of the Pacific in Los Angeles. In the ocean, the whale would very probably eat the dolphin. (Marineland of the Pacific, Los Angeles)

mistaken for his larger relative because he has the same large dorsal (back) fin. But his habits are much more peaceful. He lives on a diet of fish and cuttlefish.

The *pilot whale,* or blackfish as he is sometimes called, can easily be identified by his large, rounded forehead. He grows to a maximum of 28 feet in the North Atlantic. The species on the southern United States coast reach only 20 feet, and the Pacific species 16 feet. In captivity, he performs almost as well as the bottle-nose. Pilot whales travel in tremendous schools of hundreds and sometimes thousands, feeding on cuttlefish and fish. In captivity they eat from 45 to 60 pounds of fish a day. Totally black, they are basically night animals.

The *grampus,* or Risso's dolphin, lives far out at sea, either by himself or in small schools of up 20 animals, feeding on fish or cuttlefish. He is found worldwide and grows to a length of 13 feet.

The *common dolphin* reaches a maximum of 8½ feet. He prefers warm or temperate waters and is rarely seen north of Iceland. Large schools of these dolphins are usually found far from shore. They live primarily on fish, and weigh, on the average, around 160 pounds.

White-sided dolphins, on the Atlantic Coast, and *striped dolphins,* on the Pacific Coast, are very closely related. They grow to a length of 9 feet and live on cuttlefish and small fish such as anchovies and sauries.

Altogether, there are more than fifty kinds of dolphins, most of which we know little about.

WHAT DOLPHINS ARE LIKE

Although the dolphin's body had to change in many ways to adapt to life in the sea, it is still basically that of a land mammal. For instance, the bones in his pectoral fins, or flippers, are the same bones as those in human hands and arms. He even has five "fingers," although they are covered by his skin as though he were wearing mittens. These flippers are not used for swimming, but are useful to the dolphin for steering.

The dolphin's "hind legs" have almost completely disappeared. What survives is a small pelvis, or hip bone, embedded in flesh. It cannot be seen from the outside of his body. This pelvis is completely useless and is not even attached to his backbone any longer.

In other seagoing mammals, the hind legs have evolved into flippers that provide the power for swimming. Dolphins and the other cetaceans use their tails, called flukes, for this purpose. A fish's tail is set vertically, the top pointing toward the surface of the water. When he swims, he moves the tail from side to side. The dolphin's flukes are set horizontally, parallel to the surface. He moves them up and down like the flipper on a frogman's foot. This makes it much easier for him to swim upward and downward. Unlike the fish, a dolphin's life depends on his ability to get to the surface to breathe. He can move his flukes vertically, however, to change direction.

The front part of the dolphin's body is quite rigid. He can barely move his neck. All of his movement takes place from the

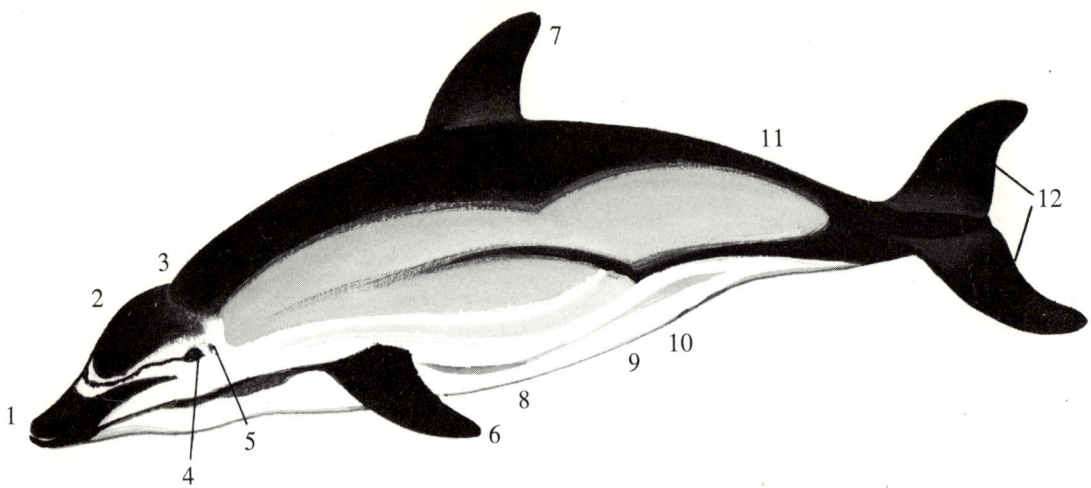

base of his tail to the end. For his size, the dolphin has more muscle than other animals. It is concentrated in his tail.

The dolphin's jutting beak, or jaw (1), is very strong. He can stun or kill a large whale or shark by ramming it with his jaw. The jaws hold eighty-eight teeth. The bulb-shaped "forehead" is called the melon (2). The blowhole (3) is on top of his head; behind it is the brain. The eye (4) is small and bright. The ear (5) is a very small hole, right behind the eye. The flipper (6), used for steering and not for swimming, corresponds to the arm and hand of humans. The dorsal fin (7) serves as a stabilizer. The dolphin has an umbilicus, or navel (8), just as humans have. The genital opening (9) and the anal opening (10) are separate in the male. The peduncle, or tail (11), is the muscular section, connecting the body to the flukes, where swimming power originates. Flukes (12) are the horizontal, flattened division of the tail.

Men have only recently begun to measure the dolphin's speed. In the open sea he seems to be moving very fast. Sailors have said that they have seen dolphins swimming as fast as fifty miles an hour. In experiments, the fastest speed measured so far has been twenty-one and a half knots (twenty-four and a half miles an hour). This record was set by a tropical dolphin of the species *Stenella*. Bottle-nose dolphins have been timed at sixteen knots (eighteen and an half miles an hour) and the striped dolphin at fifteen knots (a little over seventeen miles an hour).

One reason people thought that dolphins were able to swim faster was because they often ride the bow waves of ships. It is not understood exactly how they do this, but scientists think it is somewhat like surfboarding. The ship pushes the water before it and the dolphin catches a lift. He can then, with little effort, go just as fast as the ship. It is possible that a dolphin riding the bow waves of a ship is having fun, just as you do when you go down a slide or zoom down a snowy hill on your sled.

Even if the dolphin did not prove to swim as fast as had been thought, his speed is still quite surprising. Water puts up a great deal more resistance to a body than air does. In order to swim at fifteen knots, a dolphin must exert as much energy as a man of the same weight climbing a mountain at five miles an hour. Very few men have the strength to do this.

Striped dolphins soar through the air.
(Marineland of the Pacific, Los Angeles)

If the dolphin's body were not streamlined to lower the resistance of the water, these speeds would be impossible. To attain the same speed would require about seven times the amount of muscle that a dolphin has. He would need the energy of a man climbing a mountain at thirty miles an hour.

This streamlining makes it possible for the dolphin to swim with an efficiency of eighty-five percent. The United States Navy was impressed enough by this to launch experiments to find out how the dolphin does it, in order to design faster submarines.

The almost complete lack of hair on the dolphin also contributes to his speed. A smooth surface creates much less resistance, and the dolphin's skin is almost as smooth as glass. Even his ears are set into his body.

Land mammals developed hair because it helped to keep their body temperatures even. In the sea, hair would not help. It would just become soggy and slow the animal down. The cetacean's answer has been to develop a layer of fat under his skin. This is his insulation against the cold. It has also led to a theory that his body shape actually changes to lower resistance to the water.

Whether fat contributes to the dolphin's speed or not, it is very important to him in another way. His bones have undergone evolution, too. Land animals have very heavy bones. Their bones need to be strong because they bear the animal's weight, working against the pull of gravity. Life in the sea no longer makes this necessary. In water, an animal's specific gravity is much lower. This is why you find it so easy to float when you are in the water.

To take full advantage of this, the dolphin developed spongy bones filled with fatty tissue. This has lowered his specific gravity to one, which means that if he lies still in the water he will neither sink nor rise.

The fact that the dolphin does not have to use his energy in struggling against the pull of gravity may explain his sleeping habits. He never falls into a deep sleep as we do, but takes what might be called catnaps instead. Compared to land mammals, he sleeps only short periods, mostly at night but sometimes during the day, too, waking up frequently to breathe and to make sure that he is not in danger.

Although dolphins have dorsal (back) fins just as fish have, these fins are much less important to them. A fish's swim bladder, a sort of air-filled balloon used to maintain buoyancy as the fish rises and sinks, is located toward the bottom of his body. A fish is always in danger of turning upside down, and when he dies this is just what he does. Alive, his dorsal fin helps him to stay upright. Dolphins' lungs are placed higher in the body, right under the backbone. The only real use that the dorsal fin might have would be as a stabilizer to help the dolphin stay on course.

The weight of the legs of most land mammals causes them to sink in the water, with their noses breaking the surface. The legless dolphin floats on an even keel, with his nose underwater. This is a much more efficient position for swimming, but it would create a serious breathing problem if his nostrils were placed like those of his land-dwelling relatives. Because of the way his weight is distributed, the first part of the dolphin to break the surface is the top of his head. And that is where his nostrils are now located. The

The opening on top of the dolphin's head is the blowhole. (Marineland of the Pacific, Los Angeles)

opening is called the blowhole. Since their mouths are almost always submerged, dolphins do not use them for breathing. Like other mammals, they pant when they surface after a dive, but they pant through the blowhole rather than the mouth.

While the dolphin is underwater, his blowhole is held tightly closed. When he surfaces, he opens it and lets out his breath in an explosive burst. Tests made with a pilot whale showed that he can empty eighty-eight percent of the air in his lungs in only one second. It is this sudden blast of air, with drops of moisture, that produces the spout of the dolphin's larger relative, the whale. The whale is not squirting water, as many people think, but moisture-laden air.

With every breath, the dolphin changes from eighty to ninety percent of the air supply in his lungs. Man changes only around twelve to thirteen percent. Because the dolphin breathes so deeply, he does not have to breathe as often as land mammals do. Normally, a dolphin takes from one to six breaths a minute. Humans take from fourteen to sixteen a minute.

Since he must dive to get his food, the dolphin has to be able to hold his breath longer than most animals. The bottle-nose dolphin can stay underwater from thirteen to fifteen minutes. Few humans can hold their breath for more than two minutes. To make these dives possible, the lungs of the bottle-nose dolphin have one and a half times the capacity of the lungs of land mammals his size.

There is another reason that the dolphin is able to go for so long without breathing. When he dives, his blood circulation changes. Blood carries oxygen from his lungs to the rest of his body. To use this air supply more efficiently, circulation is cut off to the dolphin's muscles. Only the heart and brain receive an oxygen supply while the dolphin is submerged. These organs would be seriously damaged if circulation were cut off for more than a brief second. But muscles can go for longer periods without receiving fresh oxygen.

Another aid to diving is the fact that the muscles of dolphins and other cetaceans are capable of storing more oxygen than those of other mammals. The sperm whale makes dives up to an hour and fifteen minutes long. His muscles receive no fresh oxygen the whole time.

For many years scientists were puzzled because cetaceans were able to dive to great depths without suffering caisson disease, commonly called the bends. This is a serious problem for human divers, causing paralysis or death.

Air contains nitrogen as well as oxygen. Under normal air pressure, humans breathe out the nitrogen. But under the tremendous pressures of deep water, the nitrogen becomes a liquid and is absorbed into the blood. If the diver surfaces too quickly, the lowered pressure will cause the nitrogen to change back into a gas as bubbles.

You can see how this happens when you open a bottle of soda. Carbon dioxide under pressure is in the soda in liquid form. When you take the cap off, you lower the pressure. Immediately the carbon dioxide begins to escape as a gas, and bubbles start rising to the surface. If this should happen in a diver's bloodstream he could become very ill or die.

The only way to prevent the bends is to rise to the surface in stages, stopping at different levels to allow the body to adjust to the reduced pressure. This is a long process and reduces the time that a diver can work underwater.

Many theories were developed to explain why the cetaceans were not bothered with the bends. But the real reason turned out to be quite simple. The human diver must go on breathing while

If a diver surfaces too quickly, he can get the bends. (United Press International)

he is underwater. So, he is continually absorbing more nitrogen into his bloodstream. But the cetacean takes with him only the air in his lungs. He doesn't add any fresh nitrogen to his blood and is, therefore, able to come quickly to the surface without danger.

THE SENSES OF THE DOLPHIN

Animals get to know their world in surprisingly different ways. Man's most important tool in learning what is going on around him is his sense of sight. For the dog, smell is much more important than vision. The rattlesnake uses his sense of touch to find his prey. His special glands are highly sensitive to body heat at a distance.

What is the dolphin's most important sense?

Smell plays little or no part in telling the dolphin about his world. This is not because smell is useless in water. Fish have very well-developed scent detectors and put them to good use in finding their food. But a mammal in the sea would face a difficult problem in using his sense of smell.

The fish is a much more primitive animal than is a mammal. His sense of smell and taste are one and the same. He smells with his mouth. In the evolution of the mammal, these two senses became separated. A mammal detects scents with a very sensitive mucous membrane in his nose. This membrane can be damaged by dry and cold air. In land mammals, the membrane is protected because it is set far back in the nasal passages. By the time air reaches it, the air has been warmed and moistened. But a seagoing mammal would choke if water reached very far into his nasal passage. This would be a constant danger. So, smell for the dolphin simply is not a practical tool. And in the course of evolution, the dolphin has almost, if not completely, lost this sense.

Little is known about the dolphin's sense of taste. Some scientists do not believe that it can be very important to him. Most animals who, like the dolphin, gulp their food without chewing it do not have a well-developed sense of taste. The nerve to the part of the dolphin's brain that analyzes taste is quite small.

Other scientists who have worked with dolphins believe that the sense of taste might be much keener than first suspected. They point out that dolphins are often quite choosy about what kind of fish they want to eat.

There is good reason to think that the dolphin's sense of touch might be very sensitive. Like most mammals they will scratch themselves on rough surfaces, and in captivity, will beg their keepers to scrub them with a brush or squirt them with a hose. And, more important — although we do not yet understand how they do it — we know that they must be able to detect pressure very well. A diving mammal has to be able to do this or he might go so deep that he couldn't get back to the surface in time to get his next breath. So, he has to have some sort of a depth gauge. Possibly it might be the melon, the rounded bulb on his forehead, that does this job. It may contain very sensitive organs that measure pressure. Scientists know that a great many nerves are concentrated

This dolphin would not eat after a long airplane trip, so his trainers hand-feed him underwater. (Marineland of the Pacific, Los Angeles)

there. But until further studies have been made, they can only guess at their purpose.

Dolphins and porpoises have the keenest vision of all the cetaceans. This is because they feed on fish that they catch fairly near the surface, where the light is good. But life in the water made

31

The dolphin's eyes are on the sides of his head. (Marineland of the Pacific, Los Angeles)

certain changes necessary in the dolphin's way of seeing things. For instance, tears protect the eye from irritation. But tears would do the dolphin no good, for water would wash them away. This is why your eyes may itch and turn red after you have been swimming. And salt water is more irritating than fresh.

For an animal moving through water at the speed of the dolphin, this irritation would be even greater. There would be more friction on the surface of his eyeballs. Through evolution, the eyeballs of the dolphin moved farther back, to the sides of his head. His eyes do not face straight ahead, as yours do. As a result, there is much less friction. Like the rest of his body, his eyes have been streamlined.

To get this protection for his eyes, the dolphin had to give up something that land hunters have — binocular, or stereoscopic, vision. Each of your eyes sees a slightly different image of what you look at because they see it from a different angle. Your brain is able to calculate, from the degree of difference, just how far away is the thing you are looking at. Binocular vision gives you what is called depth perception, or three-dimensional vision. Unlike some cetaceans, the dolphin still has some depth perception, but his vision is binocular only when things are at a distance. As he gets closer to objects, he is less and less able to judge visually how far away they are.

Even without binocular vision, the dolphin's eyesight is good enough to let him catch fish thrown to him, jump through hoops, play ball, and even recognize individual human beings. But no matter how good his eyesight is, it is still of limited use to him in his life underwater.

Bottle-nose dolphins spend a great deal of their time in muddy water in harbors or river mouths. Vision there is almost useless because of the mud that is constantly stirred up. One close relative, the susu, a cetacean that lives in India, spends his entire life in the muddy Ganges River, where it is impossible to see anything. As a result, the susu has become almost totally blind. His eyes can do nothing more than sense light. How, then, does he manage to get around and find his food?

THE IMPORTANT SENSE OF SOUND

The answer to the susu's problem, and to the dolphin's, too, is sound. The dolphin's sense of hearing is believed to be among the most sensitive of that of all animals. But merely listening would not be enough to guide him through the darkness of the water. All it would tell him is how to locate other animals that make sounds. Of course, that would be of some help. For centuries men thought of the sea as silent. Now we know that it is full of animals making different sounds.

But the dolphin's real secret is that he makes sounds of his own. Unlike people, he uses his blowhole rather than his mouth. He has no vocal cords. The dolphin sends out signals that bounce back to him from whatever they hit.

Sound waves travel at a known speed. When the dolphin sends out a signal, he can tell how far away an object is by how quickly the echo returns. This is called echolocation or sonar (*sound navigation ranging*). The bat uses much the same method to find his way through the night, but he does not have the advantages that the dolphin has.

The dolphin sends out signals in the water. (Marineland of the Pacific, Los Angeles.)

The dolphin gets his answers much more rapidly than the bat because sound waves travel five times faster in water than in air. The speed of sound in water is about one mile per second. Sound also travels much farther in water than in air. An explosion in the ocean off Hawaii can be picked up forty minutes later by instruments in San Francisco. In that time the sound will have traveled over two thousand miles.

The sound that the dolphin uses for echolocation has been described as that made by a creaking door or rusty hinge. Actually, just like the sonar used by ships hunting submarines, it is a rapid clicking or pinging. But the dolphin has developed echolocation far beyond that which man has been able to manage until now.

What makes the dolphin's echolocation so effective is a combination of his ability to make and to hear sound in an extremely wide range of frequencies. To understand the importance of this, it is necessary to learn what sound really is.

When something vibrates — moves back and forth within a limited distance — in air or water, it sets up a kind of motion that radiates outward from it in straight lines, moving through the atmosphere. These waves of vibration are picked up by our eardrums, which are really nothing more than sensitive instruments for sensing such vibrations.

If the vibration is slow, the sound has what is called a low frequency. If it is rapid, it has a high frequency. The full range of sound is far greater than human ears are capable of detecting. There is a limit to how high a frequency we can hear. Sounds beyond our range are said to be ultrasonic. While humans cannot hear them, animals may be able to do so. You may have seen one of the "silent" dog whistles. These whistles are ultrasonic. When you blow one you cannot hear anything — but your dog can. His ear is able to hear higher frequencies than yours. But the dolphin's hearing is even sharper than a dog's, and he puts it to good use.

Frequencies are measured in the number of cycles, or sound waves, per second. This chart shows you the great difference between your ears' sensitivity and that of the dolphin.

HIGHEST FREQUENCY HEARD BY ANIMALS

Animal	*Cycles per Second*
Bat	98,000
Mouse	95,000
Dolphin	80,000
Cat	50,000
Katydid	45,000
Moth	40,000
White Rat	40,000
Dog	35,000
Chimpanzee	26,000
Human Child	23,000
Human Adult	20,000
Pigeon	10,000
Frog	10,000

The dolphin, as you can see, has a range of hearing four times greater than yours. Since he can also make sounds over a much

The dolphin's "sonar" keeps him away from objects such as glass. (Marineland of the Pacific, Los Angeles)

farther range, he is able to use different frequencies in different ways in echolocation.

Tests have shown that the dolphin can "see" with his ears just as well as you can with your eyes. A dolphin lying at rest in the water will, every fifteen or twenty seconds, send out a series of low-frequency clicks. He uses a low frequency because it travels farther than high frequencies. The sound goes out, bounces off the objects around him, and returns. When his brain analyzes what he hears, the dolphin has only a blurred impression of what is around him, but it is enough to detect any changes or any new objects.

If the dolphin does detect anything different from what his signals have shown before, he will make his creaking sound at a higher frequency. This will begin to give him a sharper focus. If what he finds "looks" like a fish, he will start toward it at top speed. As he gets closer to the object, he begins to move his head back and forth. This lets him listen stereophonically. It gives him the same effect as your stereoscopic vision gives you. It makes it possible for him to tell how far off the object is. Meanwhile, the sounds he makes keep rising into higher and higher frequencies. As they do, the picture becomes sharper and sharper.

Most of the other animals in the sea make sounds in the lower frequencies. To the dolphin, this is like static on a radio. By sending out signals in higher frequencies and listening to those, he

Blindfolding a dolphin for "sonar" tests.
(United Press International)

eliminates this static. In terms of hearing, it has the same effect that squinting has in sight. Everything you see depends on light entering your eye. But when there is too much light you lower your eyelids to reduce the light so that you can see more clearly.

What the dolphin "sees" is quite different from what your eyes would show you. In some cases, this gives him advantages that eyes would not. For example, in one test a group of dolphins was penned in. The scientists left two openings in the wire fence that surrounded them. But one opening was actually blocked by a pane of Plexiglas. A human might have bumped into it, because it would have been invisible to his eyes. The dolphins never made that mistake. The Plexiglas gave off echoes. That was all they had to know.

But echolocation is not always better than vision. Dolphins are often trapped because of it, when it would be quite simple for them to escape.

A group of Alaskan fishermen once captured a young killer whale. He was being taken to Seattle, swimming between the boats but enclosed by nets. His pack followed, trying to free him. Full-grown males, thirty feet long, would charge at the net and then turn away at the last moment. They could easily have torn through it. The problem was that, to them, it was a wall. Their echolocation showed them only a surface. It could not tell them how flimsy

it was. As far as the animals were concerned, it could have been a solid wall of concrete.

But for most purposes, the dolphin's echolocation works very well for him. He can tell the difference between fish of different types by their size. In fact, he can detect objects as small as a BB shot. He can also tell whether an object is soft or hard.

Men thought they had done something very clever when they invented sonar. Only in the last few years have they learned that nature had done the same thing long before, and had done it far better.

THE LANGUAGE OF THE DOLPHIN

The dolphin has another use for sound, one that has stirred up much argument among scientists. They do agree on one thing. The dolphin uses sound for communication. The question that no one agrees on is whether or not the dolphin has a language.

So far as we know, every higher animal has some means of communicating with others of his species. When a Virginia deer senses danger, he flicks his tail upward. The underside of the tail is completely white, the only white on the animal's body. Immediately, all the other animals in the herd are alerted. This is communication. It is not, however, language.

Prairie dogs station certain members of their community as

sentinels, to watch for danger while the others eat and play. If the watcher sees a hawk, he lets out a series of quick, shrill whistles. Every dog in the town instantly dives for his hole. If the danger is on the ground — a coyote or badger — the signal is a yip.

When the threat has passed, the first dog to see that the town is safe lets out a series of yells that sound the "all clear." Every other animal comes rushing out of his burrow and joins in the shout of joy. And the eating and romping begin again. The prairie dog can say more than the deer, but he still does not have a true language.

True language is taught to the young by the old. The deer and the prairie dog are born knowing the proper signals. The signals are instinctive. But a prairie dog, with his many signals, still does not have a language, because he does not have enough signals. For a group of signals to become a language, there must be *at least ten thousand different ideas* that can be communicated from one animal to another.

Scientists are people who demand proof. Since we have not yet managed to talk with dolphins, it is easy to see why many do not agree that the dolphin does use language.

Does the idea of talking with animals sound strange? It is not only possible, it has been done. Dr. Konrad Lorenz, an Austrian who has devoted his life to studying animals, has learned to "speak" with geese. He is able not only to understand what the birds are talking about, but he can get them to obey his orders. They will form into line and march out of their pond. He can make them go faster or slower by giving the right honks. The flock he talks with actually seem to believe that he is just another goose.

Dolphins "talk" to one another. (Marineland of the Pacific, Los Angeles)

Even if geese had brains large enough to develop a full language, its use would be difficult for them. The number of sounds they can make is just too limited. But the dolphin has no such problem. Most of his conversation is in whistles that sound like a canary's song. He can vary these by rapidly changing pitch. He can also make a wide variety of clicks, clucks, squawks, mews, quacks, and blats that sound like a Bronx cheer. So far, scientists have identified at least thirty-two different whistle patterns that are regularly used, but they have learned the meaning of only a few.

Dr. John C. Lilly, director of Communications Research Institute, is working with dolphins in the Virgin Islands and Miami, Florida. He has discovered something that may be very important in understanding how dolphins communicate. The dolphin's nostrils are divided, like those of other mammals, into two sections. There is a sound-making apparatus in each of them. Dr. Lilly observed that when the dolphin is making sounds, each of the sides of his blowhole operates independently of the other. The animal can make two different sounds at the same time. He can speak stereophonically.

Dr. Lilly developed a theory to explain how the dolphin might use this ability. Since the dolphin hears rather than sees motion, it would be important for him to be able to describe motion to others. Speaking in stereo — moving sound from one side of his blowhole to the other — he could do this very well by imitating the "Doppler effect."

The Doppler effect is something you have often heard, even though you might not have known the name for it. For instance, when a car passes you, blowing its horn, you hear the sound of the horn rise in pitch as the car gets nearer and nearer and then drop again as it goes away. The horn not only gets louder and then softer, but it sounds different. If your hearing were as well developed as the dolphin's, you could tell just how far away the source of the sound was and how fast it was moving.

This could be very important to the dolphin. There are few landmarks at sea; it would be very difficult for him to tell others where something is. But by mimicking the Doppler effect, he would be able to say how far away it was, whether it was coming closer or going away, and at what speed. The others would be able to "see" exactly what he sees.

How do dolphins use these means of communication? Two stories stand as evidence that they are able to do so in ways that give them a great advantage over most other animals.

In 1962, the United States Air Force, working with engineers from the Lockheed Aircraft Corporation, was making studies of underwater sound off the coast of Baja California, in Mexico. They were trying to find ways to make sonar more efficient for detecting submarines. The noises made by dolphins and other sea creatures created interference.

In one experiment, they placed a line of buoys across the entrance to a large lagoon. The buoys went twelve feet down into the water. They also put down two hydrophones, special microphones for picking up underwater sounds, so that they could tell what reaction came from the buoys.

Toward the end of the day they saw the dorsal fins of five Pacific bottle-noses headed toward the barrier. Almost as soon as they sighted the animals, the hydrophones picked up a sharp increase in the dolphins' clicking. They had "seen" the buoys. After a moment the animals seemed to calm down, and they moved into shallower water, gathering close together.

Soon one dolphin swam away by himself toward the barrier. He moved down the line from end to end and then returned to the group. The engineers heard loud whistling for a while, and another dolphin left for a second inspection. When he returned there was more excited whistling. Finally, cautiously, the dolphins swam toward the line of buoys and dived under it to reach the open sea.

There seems to be only one explanation for what had happened. When the dolphins detected the buoys, they recognized them as a threat — something strange and, therefore, possibly dangerous. They gathered at a safe distance and held a conference. A scout was sent out to find if there were a way around the buoys or an opening. The scout returned and reported that the buoys stretched all the way across the mouth of the lagoon.

The next question was, Could they swim under the buoys or were there nets? A second scout went out to see and came back to report that it seemed safe. Then the group made its escape.

The important thing is that the dolphins had held a conference. They had talked the situation over and decided what to do.

Another incident took place in the Antarctic, during the whaling season. A fishing fleet was being badly bothered by a huge school of thousands of killer whales. The big dolphins were killing off all the fish around the boats.

The fishermen radioed a nearby whaling fleet for help. The whalers came to their aid with several catcher boats that mounted harpoon guns. One was able to get a shot off at a killer whale.

Within half an hour, every killer within a fifty-mile area moved out of range of the harpoon guns. But whenever the catcher boats went away, the killers went right on bothering the fishermen.

If that was all there was to report, it would still be an amazing story. But there is more. The fishing boats and the catcher boats were almost exactly alike. They were both ex-Navy boats of the same type. The only difference was the harpoon gun. And that is what the dolphin who sounded the warning must have let the others know. He somehow described that single difference.

True, there is no *proof* that the dolphins use language — no scientific proof. But incidents like these make it clear that there is good reason to suspect they might.

THE YOUNG DOLPHIN

No animal would have evolved as good a means of communication as the dolphin has unless he were very social.

The dolphin *is* a social animal. Most are unhappy when alone. They travel in groups; sometimes, as with the pilot whales, these are groups of thousands.

Although we do not have any way of really knowing, what we see of dolphins makes us think that they must be very happy most of the time. Dolphins have no natural enemies other than

Dolphins seem to be happy all the time. This one, named Sandy, performs with a chimp called Chester. (Sea World)

other dolphins — the killer whales. And the killer whale has none at all.

The sea is filled with food. Again and again, wild dolphins have shown not only that they enjoy playing but that their way of life allows them plenty of time to do it. It is hard not to envy an animal on what seems to be a twelve-month vacation.

Bottle-nose dolphins mate sometime between February and April. From ten months to a year later, between the next February and March, the baby dolphins are born. Usually only one baby is born but, occasionally, there are twins and triplets.

With most mammals, babies are born headfirst. But baby dolphins are born tailfirst. A baby mammal's bloodstream is connected to his mother's until he is born. He gets his oxygen from her blood until birth. But as soon as he is able to breathe himself, he is in danger of suffocating — or, in the dolphin's case, drowning. So, the last thing to separate from the mother is the newborn dolphin's head.

He is born knowing how to swim. This is instinctive. It has to be, for a mammal born in the water. He immediately must swim to the surface for his first breath.

But dolphins do not leave this first swim to chance. Before the baby is born, when his mother is in labor and getting ready to give birth, other female dolphins gather around her. If he has trouble reaching the surface, they swim under him and carry him up until his blowhole breaks the surface.

The problem of reaching the surface is only one of many facing the young mammal born in the sea. Unlike other mammals he is not born in a snug place where his mother can warm him and take care of him. Right from the moment of his birth, a baby dolphin must be able to do a number of things for himself. In order to survive, he must be born with working eyes, ears, and other senses. He must soon be able to swim about quickly enough to keep up with the grown-ups. He has to be able to follow his mother. Almost the only thing that his mother can do for him is to give him food. Within half an hour of his birth, the baby dolphin begins to seek her mammary glands, the organs that give milk.

Any baby animal able to do all these things has to be quite large at birth. The young dolphin weighs between ten and fifteen percent of his mother's weight (or about forty pounds), between two and three times larger than the human baby in relation to his mother.

The young dolphin and his mother are very close. He stays right beside her, often swimming just behind her dorsal fin or under one of her flippers. The young bottle-nose may have an "aunt," too — the only other dolphin his mother will let near the baby at first. The baby dolphin and his mother call back and forth almost constantly as they swim. When she sleeps, baby sleeps — often under her protective tail.

When he is two weeks old, the calf, as the baby is called, may become a little more independent, swimming away from his mother or aunt. So long as he stays with the school, or herd, he has little to worry about. Other adults will protect him, and they seem to enjoy his company. Dolphins love to play, even as they grow older, and the baby dolphin is full of fun. Often other females will "borrow" him from his mother just to have a chance to play with a calf. Even the most serious old bull (a grown male) cannot long resist

a youngster who wants to frolic, and will often join him for a game.

Although sharks will attempt to attack young dolphins, they are rarely a problem. So long as the baby sticks close to the grown-ups, he is safe. No matter how dangerous the shark may be to human beings, for dolphins he is easy to handle. They can swim faster then the shark can; they have senses superior to his; and they have a brain so much more advanced that the shark really hasn't a chance.

Dolphins have a standard tactic for dealing with any shark that seems to want a young dolphin for his meal. One or more of the school will swim out to attract the shark's attention. The slow-witted shark will turn to the attack. Meanwhile, other dolphins will have moved in on either side of him. While the shark watches his intended victim, the dolphins launch the attack. Charging in at high speed, they slam their hard beaks into his side, crushing his gills. In a short time, the shark has drowned and the baby is safe. The dolphins can go back to living their normal lives.

But not all strangers are unwelcome. Other species of dolphins, and their relatives the whales, may cruise along with them for a while. Some scientists believe that there may be a common language which many of these cousins can use to communicate.

When he is between five and seven months old, the young dolphin will eat his first fish. This is not easy for him. He may spit

A baby dolphin stays close to his mother.
(Marineland of the Pacific, Los Angeles)

Sharks will sometimes try to attack baby dolphins. (United Press International)

it up while his mother rubs his sore stomach with her nose. Now he is on his way to becoming an adult and will soon be able to feed himself and become a full-fledged member of dolphin society.

DOLPHIN SOCIETY

From what men have been able to observe of dolphin life in captivity — and most animals are at their worst in captivity — their society is generally full of good will. While they are having conversations, for example, the animals show courtesy that is rare among human beings. Each has his own whistling cry to identify himself, so that the others will know who is speaking. So long as he talks, no other dolphin will interrupt.

The young dolphin soon learns that there are rules he must obey. Each school has what is a called a "pecking order," in which each animal has social status. Some dolphins are more important in this order than others. And they prove this in fights, leaving tooth marks on one another, lashing out with their tails, and butting with their beaks. Fights during the mating season can be quite vicious.

But at other times they are careful to look out for one another. One of the identified dolphin speech patterns is the call for help. As soon as it is given, other animals rush to the aid of the

Dolphins love to play. (Marineland of the Pacific, Los Angeles)

dolphin in distress. The most frequent reason that a dolphin calls for help is, naturally for a mammal, because he is unable to breathe. He cannot rise to the surface as the result of illness or injury. None of the others waste any time discussing this. They know it is a serious problem. Immediately they swim under him, one on each side under his flippers, and carry him to the surface.

So long as he is ill, his nurses will stay with him. And this is not easy for them. While they are carrying him, they themselves are unable to breathe as they normally would. One has to take turns going up for breaths while the other supports the sick animal from below.

Strangely, while all bottle-noses will respond in this way, some of the other dolphins, such as the common dolphin, will immediately flee from an animal in trouble, sensing that they might place themselves in danger by helping.

There seems to be an instinctive drive in the dolphin to push things to the surface. In captivity, it is an important part of their play. The young animals will spend hours carrying things to the surface and then letting them sink again so that they can repeat the game. Almost all animal play is, in one way or another, useful practice for things that will be important to the animal in later life.

This instinct undoubtedly developed so that the animals would do a better job of cooperating for the good of the species. But it has played an important role in their dealings with another animal, too. Man.

MAN MEETS DOLPHIN

Although men have only recently begun to study dolphins in a scientific manner, man's relationship with these animals goes back a long, long way.

Almost two thousand years ago, Pliny the Elder, a Roman scholar who liked to write about natural history — in fact, he met his death while trying to observe an eruption of the volcano Vesuvius too closely — wrote a story that was already an old tale when he heard it. It was the story of the friendship between a young boy and a dolphin. The boy fed the dolphin from his hand, and on school days the dolphin gave him a ride across the bay to Pozzuoli and back home again at the end of the day.

Many ancient cups, coins, and urns were decorated with figures of dolphins. The ancient Greeks and Romans held the dolphin in high regard, and even thought that dolphins were the descendants of humans who had chosen to live in the sea. Many of their tales were dismissed as legends. Then, in recent times, newspaper and magazine stories began to tell about dolphins and humans meeting on friendly terms. It seems as if people of the ancient world were well aware that the dolphin was a remarkable animal, and that modern man is only now rediscovering it.

Not very long ago, in New Zealand, children made friends with a dolphin they named Opo. For many summers this dolphin played games with them near the shore and occasionally gave them rides.

There are two ways to be given a ride by a dolphin. One way

A trainer takes a ride on Shamu, 4,000 pounds and the world's first performing killer whale. (Sea World)

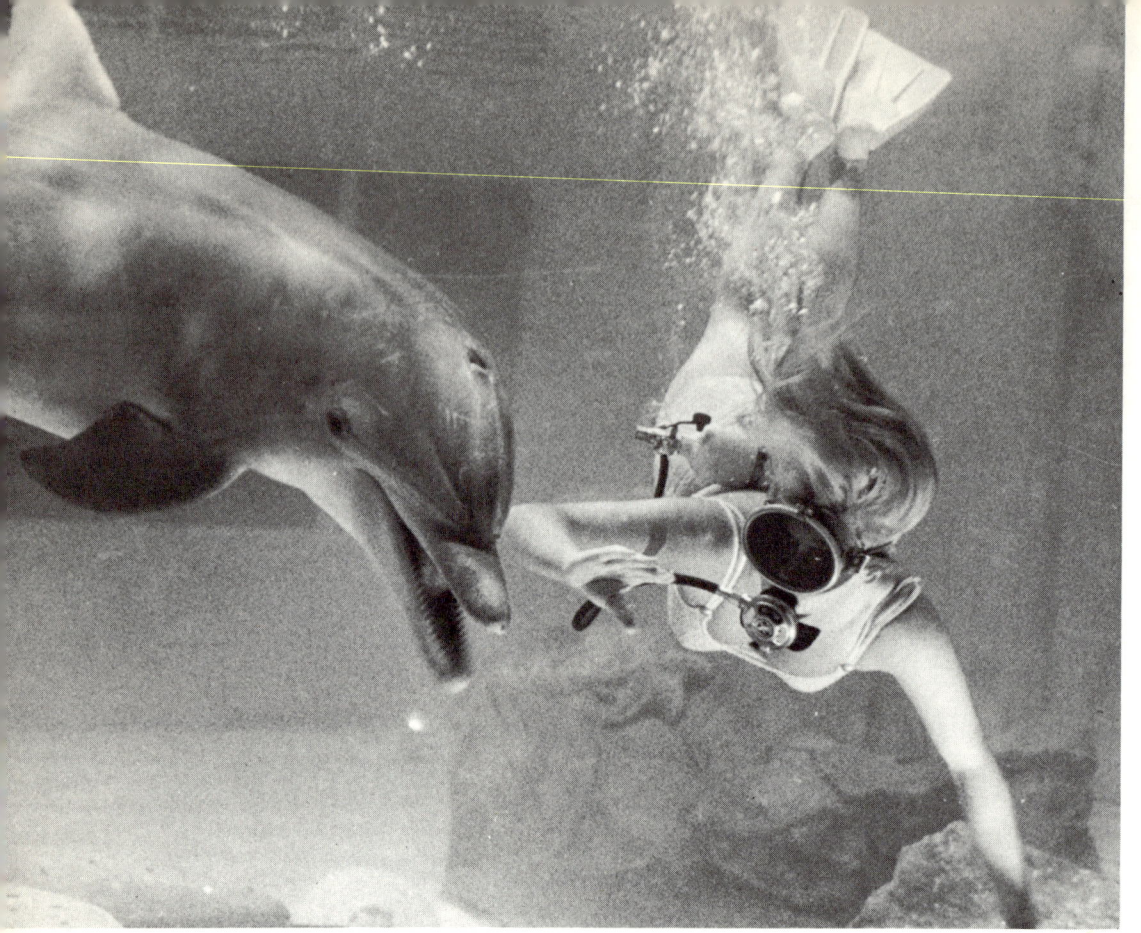

Dolphins are friendly and curious. (Sea World)

is to hold on to his dorsal fin and be towed through the water. Opo liked to come into shallow water, dive between the feet of a child, lift him up on her "shoulder" for a short spin, and then dump him gently into the water a few yards away. However, no dolphin likes to be held by his tail flukes. That is where his "motor power" comes from.

There are many, many modern stories about dolphins who have been friendly and helpful to humans — dolphins who have helped fishermen by herding fish into their nets (and have been rewarded with a share of the catch); dolphins who have guided ships safely into harbors; and even dolphins who have saved the lives of swimmers in trouble, by pushing them toward the shore.

Why are dolphins so friendly? One reason may be that dolphins have no natural enemies and, therefore, are not suspicious and wary by nature. Another reason is that dolphins are naturally curious. They approach and investigate boats, people, and floating objects.

They are inquisitive about everything that goes on around them. This may be due partly to intelligence and partly to the fact that the dolphin is carnivorous (meat-eating). Animals that have to find and capture their food are more lively and inventive than animals that are herbivorous (plant-eating) and can just walk up to their dinner of grass or leaves.

PERFORMING DOLPHINS

Have you ever seen a dolphin performing tricks in an aquarium? There are several aquariums or oceanariums in the United States. Most of them are in Florida and California, where the capture and transporting of dolphins do not present serious problems.

A 500-pound bottle-nose clears the 18-foot-high bar. (Marineland of the Pacific, Los Angeles)

Dolphins have unexpectedly become the main attraction at aquariums. Originally, these places were built to display collections of marine life, especially rare and brilliant fish that most people do not ordinarily see in their own habitat. A few dolphins were included in the collections.

The dolphins soon began to steal the show. They were so lively and playful that they invented their own games and invited spectators to play with them. They would bring up rocks and shells from the pool bottom and flip them to visitors. They would turn a bird's feather or a paper cup into a toy and play with it by the hour. If anybody threw them a ball, they would catch it and throw it back. The aquarium staffs suddenly realized that they were in show business!

Some of the tricks in the dolphins' performances are playing baseball, basketball, and tenpins; jumping through hoops; blowing trumpets; jumping out of the water and spinning around; tail-walking; "singing"; and performing synchronized water "ballets."

Dolphins are taught by a system of rewards. If a captured dolphin is a naturally good jumper, for instance, he is rewarded with a fish for jumping higher and higher — sometimes twelve feet or more into the air. And dolphins learn from each other. A new tank mate will learn tricks from an old hand and collect his share of the rewards.

SCIENTISTS BECOME CURIOUS

As dolphins began to show what they could do — carrying out commands, learning routines, and even imitating human speech in a high-pitched, ducklike manner — scientists began to show an interest in studying this little-known marine mammal.

They wanted to find out as much as possible about his large and complex brain. The scientists wanted to find out whether the many sounds made by a dolphin are really a form of language, and whether we can communicate with him. They wanted to find out more about oceanography from him — what he knows about navigation, ocean currents, the migration of fish. Some scientists became so interested that they have made the study of dolphins their major field of work.

Because their showmanship and popularity now made it economically possible to catch and transport dolphins to specially built tanks, and also made it possible to pay for their food and care, dolphins became available for the first time for scientists to study firsthand.

A veterinarian inspects a dolphin's mouth. (U.S. Navy)

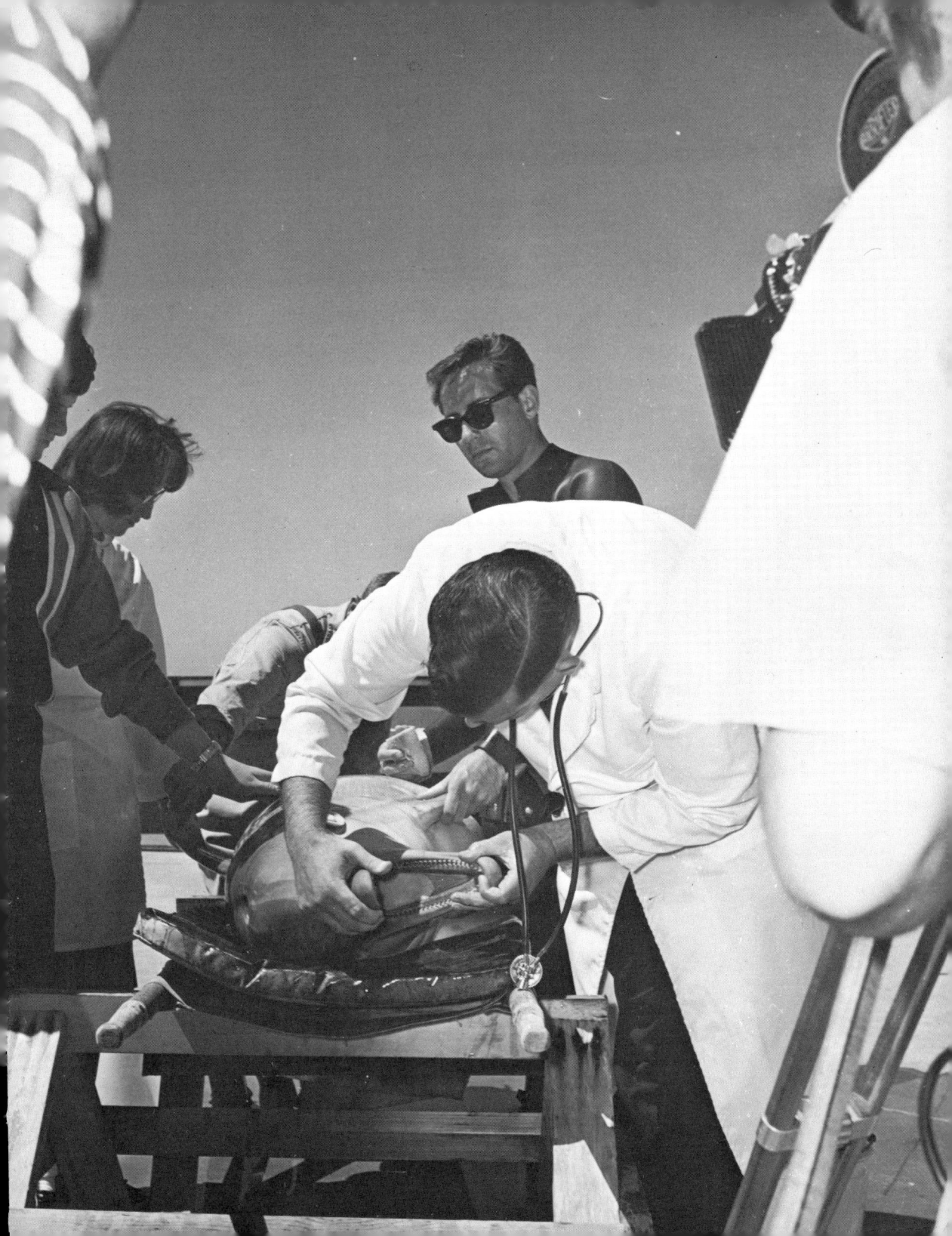

A DOLPHIN JOINS THE NAVY

Some of the early funds for research were provided by the United States Navy. The Navy wanted to find out how the dolphin's sonar works. The Navy also wanted to learn more about the dolphin's shape and speed in water, so that improvements could be made in the design of torpedoes and submarines.

Tuffy gets ready for his tests. (U.S. Navy)

One dolphin joined the Navy's undersea experimental program, Sealab II. Tuffy, a seven-foot bottle-nose, was trained to carry messages and equipment to aquanauts in experimental rescues.

HOW TO CATCH A DOLPHIN

It is very hard to catch a dolphin without injuring him. And it is hard to keep him alive during transportation. Out of water, an element in which a dolphin is weightless, the pressure of gravity and the weight of his body make it difficult for his muscles to fill and empty his lungs.

Capture is usually carried out in a shallow area of the sea, when it is calm and the visibility is good. Sometimes dolphins are caught in narrow rivers as the tide runs out. Sometimes they are rescued from sandbars where they have stranded themselves.

In the sea, a very long net is dropped from boats around a herd of dolphins, then gathered tighter and tighter. The catchers want healthy young dolphins, but they try not to separate a baby dolphin from its mother. They must handle the animals very carefully, for their flippers are delicate and easily bruised.

They are moved carefully in slings or tanks. Often the tanks are lined with foam rubber. The dolphins' delicate skin must be kept wet or it will crack and become infected.

Dolphins must be handled very carefully. (United Press International)

Captured and transported to the laboratory pools, many dolphins seemed to look on with great interest as scientists began to devise tests to discover how intelligent the dolphin really is.

HOW INTELLIGENT IS THE DOLPHIN?

It is not easy to try to understand an intelligence different from our own. The same standards do not apply. Humans live in a world of sight. Our eyes tell us a great deal of what we know about the world. We also have a very important appendage, the thumb, which is opposable — capable of being placed opposite something. We learn about objects through handling, or manipulating, them. We change our world by using tools.

Dolphins live in a world where the most important sense is the sense of sound. It is highly developed and tells them most of what they need to know about their environment.

It is very hard for man to measure the intelligence even of his own species. You probably realize that the tests you take to rate your knowledge or ability would not be very good for testing an Eskimo boy or girl or a young Bushman. They would not even be a good test for a young French student, unless the language were changed. But how much harder it is to test a creature whose whole frame of reference is entirely different!

These are some experiments that were thought up by scientists for testing various abilities of dolphins. Can you think of some tests that would demonstrate what dolphins can do? What equipment would you use to conduct your tests?

In a laboratory test, a dolphin was trained to push a lever to activate an electronic signal to an electrode implanted in the "pleasure-producing" center of the brain. Monkeys require several hundred trials to learn this task. Some of the tested dolphins have

managed it in twenty trials or less — almost as fast as a human can learn. This indicates that a dolphin's "thought processes" are extremely fast.

Invisible obstructions, such as sheets of glass or plastic, were lowered into a dolphin tank. A hydrophone (a special microphone for detecting underwater sounds) was put into the tank. After touching a few of the obstacles, the dolphins in the tank adapted to a swimming pattern that avoided them, even at night. Dolphins used their echolocation — not eyes or sense of touch — to locate and avoid these obstacles.

The hydrophone shows us that dolphins are aware every time a foreign object is dropped into their pool. Dolphins put out a steady, simple ticking for general reconnaissance. When something is dropped into the pool, the sound changes into a rusty-hinge sound and continues until the dolphin has discovered the size and position of the object. Even an object as small as a single BB shot (11/64 of an inch in diameter) is noticed and checked.

Two dolphins were taught to push underwater levers to earn a fish. A steady light signaled, "Push the button on the right"; a flashing light signaled, "Push the button on the left." The dolphins quickly mastered this trick. They were then taught to do it in order, with the same dolphin going first each time. Finally, a partition was set up between the two. Only one dolphin — the one who always went second — could see the signal light. When she saw it, she

Scientists want to know how intelligent the dolphin really is.
This bottle-nose seems interested in getting to know the tiny Yorkshire terrier.
(Marineland of the Pacific, Los Angeles)

gave a burst of sound — and the dolphin behind the partition pushed the correct button. This test indicates that dolphins can communicate specific information to each other.

In carrying out tests on dolphins, scientists have sometimes become aware that they themselves are being tested by their subjects. Dr. John Lilly was conducting a test in which he rewarded a dolphin for giving a whistle of a definite pitch, length, and loudness. The dolphin began to give the whistle at varying pitches, some going into the supersonic range, which Dr. Lilly could not hear. When the dolphin received no fish (the reward) for whistles above a certain frequency, he returned to the scientist's acoustic range for the rest of the experiment. The dolphin had tested the human's range of hearing, established what the upper limit was, and, thereafter, stayed within it to earn his reward.

THE DOLPHIN'S BRAIN

The brain of an adult dolphin (eight feet long and weighing 300 pounds) weighs about 1,700 grams. An adult 150-pound man's brain weighs about 1,459 grams. So, the dolphin's brain weighs

A dolphin gets to know his trainer.
(Marineland of the Pacific, Los Angeles)

about 250 grams more than man's. (A gram is a unit of weight and mass equal to one thousandth of a kilogram. The kilogram is a little over two pounds.)

HOW MUCH DO BRAINS WEIGH?

Adult Animal	Average Brain (in grams)
Mouse	0.4
Guinea Pig	4.8
Cat	31.0
Dog	65.0
Chimpanzee	350.0
Gorilla	450.0
Man	1,450
Dolphin	1,700
Elephant	6,075
Sperm Whale	9,200

Weight is not the only way of judging a brain, however. The ratio of brain weight to body weight is important. The elephant, for instance, has a brain that may weigh 6,075 grams — but the elephant is fifty-four feet long. Much of his big brain is involved in managing the functions of his huge body.

But both man and dolphin have relatively large brains in relation to the size of their bodies.

RATIO OF BODY WEIGHT TO BRAIN WEIGHT

Animal	Body Weight (in pounds)	Brain Weight (in pounds)	Brain Weight Compared to Body Weight
Man	150	3.1	2.1%
Dolphin	300	3.5	1.17%
Chimpanzee	110	0.77	0.70%
Elephant	12,000	11.0	0.12%

These are other characteristics by which we judge a brain:

• The complexity of the brain — both man and dolphin have complex folds, fissures, and convolutions on the brain's surface.

• The cell density of the brain — both man and dolphin have a high nerve-cell count.

• The number of layers in the cortex (outer part) of the brain — rats and rabbits have four layers of cell types; monkeys, men, and dolphins have six.

The brain of the dolphin looks rather like two boxing gloves placed side by side. It is wider than it is long — just the opposite of the brains of other animals. This leads many scientists to suppose that the auditory portion of the brain — the part concerned with receiving and analyzing sound — may be larger and more complex than in other animals, and that, therefore, the dolphins have a much better developed sense of sound than other animals have.

Scientists have begun to dissect, study, and map the brain of the dolphin. In dissection, scientists cut apart tissues and study the structure and the cells of the brain in very small sections.

Techniques have also been developed in mapping the living brain, to find what areas control various functions. In this process, scientists expose the brain of a living animal and find out which areas motivate the animal to feel pleasure and which areas control feelings of pain or distress. By implanting electrodes in the brain and then stimulating different areas, scientists can produce different feelings during testing situations. Using this system, a dolphin (or any other animal) can be tested, using a very direct punishment-and-reward system, to discover how much and how fast he can learn.

CURRENT RESEARCH ON DOLPHINS

Many tests on dolphins, repeated in laboratories under scientific rules, are rapidly adding to our knowledge. You might watch for

Dolphins enjoy play for its own sake.
(Marineland of the Pacific, Los Angeles)

newspaper and magazine articles that will keep you up-to-date on the latest results of such experiments.

This new knowledge has led so far to the following observations:

- The dolphin has a wider range of capabilities than just those necessary for survival.
- Learning for dolphins is very rapid and requires little trial-and-error time.
- Dolphins enjoy play for its own sake — not for rewards.
- A degree of reasoning seems to be present in some testing situations.

Much of the research on the brain of the dolphin — research that is still in the early stages — raises as many questions as it answers. Just how intelligent is the dolphin? What does he use his large and complex brain for? Is he intelligent in any way that we can understand and relate to, or is he doing something else, something entirely different, from what we do with our brains?

The dolphin's large brain does not necessarily mean that he possesses intellect. It does not necessarily mean that he will ever talk to us, either in our own language or, through computers, in his system of sounds.

The dolphin remains a mystery. The next few years may bring amazing answers to the questions we are now asking.

CONVERSATION WITH A DOLPHIN

Dr. Lilly, who has been studying the dolphin at special laboratories, begins his book *Man and Dolphin* in this way:

"Within the next decade or two the human species will establish communication with another species: nonhuman, alien, possibly extraterrestrial, more probably marine; but definitely highly intelligent, perhaps even intellectual."

The idea of communicating with another species is exciting in itself. You have read the life stories of humans who live in other countries and of those who have lived in other centuries. Think of learning the life story of another species — his experiences, his philosophy, his memories — from his own point of view!

Dr. Lilly reminds us of other benefits of this breakthrough. What we will have learned about communicating will help people in communicating with each other — an area where misunderstandings arise often enough between parent and child, between people of one background and another, and between people of one country and another.

Another benefit — and one not beyond the bounds of imagination — is that in the process of learning to talk with another earthly species, we will be preparing ourselves to talk to extraterrestrial forms of intelligence. As astronauts reach farther and farther into space, it becomes more likely that someday, somewhere in outer space, we will make contact with some form of life.

As our knowledge of the universe becomes more sophisticated,

Will man one day communicate with this friendly creature? (United Press International)

we may monitor some form of signals from another galaxy. Will we have the skill we need to decipher these signals? What we learn about communication from dolphins may help us to be prepared.

What will this new knowledge bring to us, besides these advantages? It may bring responsibilities. It may make us acknowledge the possibility that we have no right to kill dolphins; to capture them and put them on display; to pollute the part of the earth in which they live. We may have to adjust our thinking quite radically — we who have always assumed ourselves to be alone at the top of the evolutionary ladder.

INDEX

Ancestors of dolphins, 6-8, 11
Aquariums, 61-63
Archaeocetes, 7, 8

Baleen, 8
Bends, 27
Blackfish. *See* Pilot whale
Blowhole, 25, 26, 45, 50
Bottle-nose dolphin, 12, 21, 33, 57, 67
Brain of dolphin. *See* Intelligence

Carnivores, 8
Catching dolphins, 67, 68
Cetacea, 7
Characteristics of dolphins, 19-29
Classification of dolphins, 4
Common dolphin, 18

Communication with dolphins, 3, 64, 79, 81. *See also* Language of dolphin
Communications Research Institute, 45

Delphinidae, 8
Dolphin society, 55-57
Dolphins
    ancestors of, 6-8, 11
    bottle-nose, 12, 21, 33, 57, 67
    characteristics of, 19-29
    classification of, 4
    common, 18
    false killer, 15, 18
    food, 12-18
    Grampus, 18

  intelligence, 3, 69-76
  language, 3, 42-48
  pilot whale, 18
  senses, 29-42
  striped, 18, 21
  white-sided, 18
  young, 6, 48-55
Dolphins and man, 58-61
Dolphins as social animals, 48
Doppler effect, 45, 46

Echolocation. See Sound sense in dolphins
Experiments with dolphins, 3, 21, 23, 26, 38, 40, 45-48, 64, 66, 67, 69-76
Eyesight of dolphins, 31-34

False killer, 15, 18
Fins, 19, 20, 24
Flippers, 19
Flukes, 19, 21
Food, dolphin, 12-18

Grampus, 18

Hydrophone, 71

Intelligence, dolphin, 3, 69-76

Killer whale, 14, 15, 47, 48, 50

Language of dolphin, 3, 42-48, 53, 64, 79, 81
Lilly, Dr. John C., 45, 73, 79
Lorenz, Dr. Konrad, 43

Mammals, 4, 6, 7, 23
Man and Dolphin, 79
Marineland, Florida, 12
Melon, 20, 30
Mysticetes, 8

Nurses, dolphin, 57

Odontocetes, 8

Performing dolphins, 61-63
Phocaenidae, 8
Pilot whale, 18
Play, dolphins' love of, 51, 57, 63
Pliny the Elder, 58
Porpoises, 7, 8, 11, 12

Research on dolphins, 76, 78
Risso's dolphin. See Grampus

Sealab II, 67
Senses of dolphins, 29-42
Sharks, as dolphin enemies, 53
Smell sense in dolphins, 29, 30
Sonar. See Sound sense in dolphins
Sound sense in dolphins, 34-42
Sperm, whale, 8, 27
Striped dolphin, 18, 21
Susu, 33
Swimming speed of dolphins, 21, 23

Taste sense in dolphins, 30
Toothed, whale, 8
Touch sense in dolphins, 30, 31
Tuffy, dolphin, 68

United States Navy, 23, 67

Vertebrates, 4

Whales, 7, 8

Sperm, 8, 27
Toothed, 8
White-sided dolphin, 18

Young dolphins, 6, 48-55